I0426040

Landsat-based Monitoring of Landscape Dynamics at Voyageurs National Park, 2002-2007

Natural Resource Technical Report NPS/GLKN/NRTR—2010/356

Alan A. Kirschbaum and Ulf B. Gafvert

National Park Service
Great Lakes Inventory and Monitoring Network
2800 Lake Shore Drive, East
Ashland, WI   54806

July 2010

U.S. Department of the Interior
National Park Service
Natural Resource Program Center
Fort Collins, Colorado

The National Park Service, Natural Resource Program Center publishes a range of reports that address natural resource topics of interest and applicability to a broad audience in the National Park Service and others in natural resource management, including scientists, conservation and environmental constituencies, and the public.

The Natural Resource Technical Report Series is used to disseminate results of scientific studies in the physical, biological, and social sciences for both the advancement of science and the achievement of the National Park Service mission. The series provides contributors with a forum for displaying comprehensive data that are often deleted from journals because of page limitations.

All manuscripts in the series receive the appropriate level of peer review to ensure that the information is scientifically credible, technically accurate, appropriately written for the intended audience, and designed and published in a professional manner. Data in this report were collected and analyzed using methods based on an established, peer-reviewed protocol and were analyzed and interpreted within the guidelines of the protocol.

Views, statements, findings, conclusions, recommendations, and data in this report do not necessarily reflect views and policies of the National Park Service, U.S. Department of the Interior. Mention of trade names or commercial products does not constitute endorsement or recommendation for use by the U.S. Government.

This report is available from the Great Lakes Inventory and Monitoring Network (http://science.nature.nps.gov/im/units/GLKN/monitor/landuse/landuse.cfm) and the Natural Resource Publications Management website (http://www.nature.nps.gov/publications/nrpm/nrtr.cfm#2010).

Please cite this publication as:

NPS 172/105049, July 2010

Contents

Figures

Tables

Abstract

Voyageurs National Park (VOYA) is located in far northern Minnesota on the border with Canada and at the southern range of numerous plant and animal communities of the boreal ecosystem. Disturbances, or distinct changes in vegetative cover, are an important part of how this ecosystem functions at the southern edge of its range. Monitoring these disturbances through time will provide information regarding historic disturbance regimes compared to present and future conditions and trends. For this analysis, disturbances in and around VOYA were delineated for six years, 2002-2007, using a combination of Landsat satellite imagery and high resolution aerial photos. We employed a set of computer algorithms, collectively known as LandTrendr, in conjunction with a dense time series of Landsat imagery to track vegetation changes in and around the park. Disturbance agents such as fire, forest harvest, development, flooding due to beaver activity, and blowdowns were attributed to each disturbance, in addition to the year of occurrence, and starting and ending vegetation classes. LandTrendr was used to identify apparent disturbances, after which high resolution imagery (e.g., airphotos, Quickbird) was used for photo interpretation to substantiate evidence of a disturbance, and hence, validate whether the disturbance occurred. Summary analyses showed that disturbances outside the park were dominated by forest harvest, while inside the park disturbances were most often caused by beaver, blowdowns, or fire. After relativizing the data, the areas adjacent to VOYA in Canada and MN experienced 10 and six times more disturbance, respectively, than inside the park.

Acknowledgments

We would like to acknowledge park staff at Voyageurs National Park for assistance in aerial photo acquisition, providing on-the-ground knowledge of land cover changes, logistical support, and in helping to design the land cover monitoring program's scope and extent for the park.

The team at Oregon State University has been instrumental in the development of the GLKN land use / land cover program, by providing assistance and guidance in development of the land cover monitoring protocol and in the implementation of the LandTrendr methods in land cover change detection.

We would also like to thank Bill Route, Steve Windels, and Mark Hart for reviewing and providing useful comments which have greatly improved the report.

Abbreviations, Acronyms, and Technical Terms Used in This Report

APFO
: Aerial Photography Field Office: a United States Department of Agriculture (USDA) Farm Service Agency (FSA) office located in Salt Lake City, UT. This office stores a large amount of aerial photography, among many other types of data. http://www.fsa.usda.gov/FSA/apfoapp?area=apfohome&subject=landing&topic=landing

B&W
: Black and white: in this report it refers to the airphoto type and was more commonly used prior to the 1990s.

CIR
: Color infrared: in this report it refers to the electromagnetic spectrum the airphotos capture, i.e., the 'true color' portion of the spectrum (red, green, blue) and the infrared portion. However, CIR film can only capture three bands of information at one time, which is most commonly green, red, and infrared.

DEM
: Digital elevation model: a digital representation of ground surface topography or terrain.

Electromagnetic spectrum
: The range of all possible frequencies of electromagnetic radiation. The electromagnetic spectrum of an object is the characteristic distribution of electromagnetic radiation emitted or absorbed by that particular object.

EOSD
: Earth Observation for Sustainable Development of forests: Canadian agency using space technologies to create products for forest inventory. Landsat imagery was used to create this land cover dataset. http://cfs.nrcan.gc.ca/subsite/eosd

ETM+
: Enhanced Thematic Mapper plus: one of the Earth observing sensors introduced into the Landsat program, located on the Landsat 7 http://landsat.usgs.gov/

GIS
: Geospatial Information System: any system that captures, stores, analyzes, manages, and presents data that are linked to location.

IKONOS
: High resolution satellite sensor owned and operated by GeoEye. It has a panchromatic band with 1 m resolution with four additional bands (B, G, R, IR) at 4 m resolution. http://www.geoeye.com/CorpSite/

Landsat
: In this report it refers to the Landsat satellite family, and more specifically to either Landsat 5 (launched in 1984) or Landsat 7 (launched in 1999), both with 30 m pixels (resolution). http://landsat.gsfc.nasa.gov/about/

MNDNR	Minnesota Department of National Resources
MS	Multispectral: in this report it refers to any imagery which contains more than three spectral bands
NAIP	National Agriculture Imagery Program: acquires aerial imagery during the agricultural growing seasons in the continental U.S. It commonly has 1 m resolution. http://www.fsa.usda.gov/FSA/apfoapp?area=home&subject=prog&topic=nai
NAPP	National Aerial Photography Program: an interagency Federal effort coordinated by the USGS which uses NAPP products to revise maps. In this report it refers to a particular set of imagery circa 1987. The NAPP program replaced the National High Altitude Photography (NHAP) program which was initiated in 1980. http://eros.usgs.gov/#/Guides/napp
NLCD	National Land Cover Data: created by USGS to produce a consistent land cover map for the U.S using Landsat imagery. Currently there are two NLCD datasets, one characterizing land cover in 1990, the other for year 2001, with another (2006) to be released in the near future. http://www.mrlc.gov/
NVCS	National Vegetation Classification System: a scheme for classifying the vegetation of the United States, maintained by NatureServe. http://biology.usgs.gov/npsveg/nvcs.html
Panchromatic	Incorporates all wavelengths of visible light.
RGB	Red, green, and blue: sometimes referred to as 'true color', it is the portion of the electromagnetic spectrum the film, or sensor, is quantifying.
SLC	Scan Line Corrector: device on-board the Landsat 7 (ETM+) satellite which compensates for the forward motion of the spacecraft so that the resulting scans are aligned parallel to each other.
SLC-off	Scan Line Corrector – off: this device failed on 31 May 2003, creating data gaps in each Landsat 7 (ETM+) image acquired after 31 May 2003.
SPOT	Satellite Pour l'Observation de la Terre: operated by Spot Image based in Toulouse, France. It has bands in the red, near-infrared, and short-wave infrared portions of the spectrum with 10 m resolution, and a panchromatic band with 5 m resolution. http://www.spot.com/
TM	Thematic Mapper: one of the Earth observing sensors introduced into the Landsat program, located on the Landsat 5 satellite. http://en.wikipedia.org/wiki/Thematic_mapper

Introduction

The Great Lakes Inventory and Monitoring Network (hereafter GLKN or Network) implemented land cover change monitoring at Voyageurs National Park (VOYA) in 2009. Landscape dynamics was ranked among the top five indicators of change for National Parks in the Great Lakes region (Route and Elias 2007). Voyageurs is the first of the nine parks in the Network to be completed under the recently developed landscape dynamics monitoring protocol (Kennedy et al. 2010).

The Network's land cover monitoring program went through consideration of remote sensing and field techniques, testing and revising methods, assessing costs and feasibility, and resulted in a protocol that is realistic both in terms of costs and staff time that should provide valuable information for understanding and managing the changing landscape within and adjacent to the nine parks.

Monitoring landscape dynamics was split into two different program directions during the vital signs ranking process, a 'coarse scale' and 'fine scale' approach. The coarse scale approach included monitoring human population and infrastructure data, (roads, housing, population), using existing datasets such as U.S. Census data, and monitoring land cover that could be detected using Landsat or similar satellite remote sensing platform. The fine scale approach included monitoring small scale changes in land cover, such as individual housing development, stream channel migration, or bluff erosion along lakeshores.

Recognizing that landscape dynamics ranked highly at virtually all of the Networks, the National Inventory and Monitoring (I&M) Program has undertaken much of the 'coarse scale' approach, including roads (Svancara et al. 2009b), past and current human population and housing (Svancara et al. 2009a), and available land cover classification data (Svancara and Story 2009). The data from the National Program, known as NPScape, has been provided to all parks in the Network and this data will continue to be updated on an annual basis. We are not reporting on the results from NPScape in this report, but may incorporate such data in the future, pending further analysis.

Earlier land cover monitoring efforts at GLKN were focused on change detection based on comparing classification of land cover at various time intervals, and/or comparing spectral values in satellite imagery to detect change. The Network sought to develop methods to update recent, detailed National Vegetation Classification System (NVCS) mapping products using two alternative methods. Both involved aggregating the detailed alliance level polygons to the coarser, formation level, and either manually reclassifying areas of apparent change using high resolution aerial photography, or building a classification using Landsat satellite imagery, or other high altitude image source. These methods proved infeasible due to the requirement of ground-based fieldwork to train photo-interpretation, build the classification, and complete an accuracy assessment. In addition, these methods commonly achieve less than 80% accuracy, which was determined to be inadequate.

We have now adopted methods based on remote sensing to identify changes in land cover and its causal agent, rather than attempting to revise and update a land cover classification. The method employs the use of a suite of remote sensing algorithms, collectively termed 'LandTrendr,' which exploits the 25-year archive of Landsat satellite imagery in defining changes in spectral trajectories in the imagery over time (Kennedy et al. In review). A very similar technique and set of algorithms which also incorporates the Landsat archive has been developed by Huang et al. (2010). We have chosen to implement LandTrendr due to the ability to modify the outputs to accommodate the user's needs and the ability to create cloud-free composite images from multiple cloudy images in a growing season. In our implementation we have selected six years as the return interval and was chosen for multiple reasons. Ecologically, this is a reasonable time span to capture the types of disturbances the Network and parks are interested in tracking and is also a reasonable sampling interval for monitoring landscape disturbances with medium resolution satellite imagery such as Landsat (Kennedy et al. 2009, Kennedy et al. 2010). Finally, this coincides with the vegetation monitoring program which samples all parks on a six year basis (Sanders et al. 2008).

Following LandTrendr analysis, Network staff manually review and validate each of these 'change' delineations (a LandTrendr output) using a variety of tools, including high resolution air photos, satellite imagery, spectral trajectories, and, if necessary, field visits. This validation includes determining the change, or disturbance agent, which can include fire, blowdown, flooding due to beaver activity or anthropogenic disturbances such as development, logging or agriculture.

As previously mentioned, a detailed vegetation map was produced using high resolution aerial photography flown in 1996. This vegetation map and methodology has been summarized and analyzed (Faber-Langendoen et al. 2007) and as such, will not be included in this report. Instead, the focus of this report will be to present summary statistics of land cover change (disturbances) over a period of six years (2002 to 2007) for three areas: Voyageurs National Park, an adjacent area in Canada, and an adjacent area in the U.S. The adjacent U.S. area is roughly a 3 km buffer around the park in Minnesota (MN) and nearly 6 km in Canada due to the large water area directly adjacent to the park to the north.

Previous Landscape Dynamic Studies in the Upper Great Lakes Region

Previous landscape change studies have focused on large-scale changes in land cover / land use using moderate resolution imagery such as Landsat with 30 m pixels. Wolter et al.(2006) examined land use and land cover change in the U.S. Great Lakes basin for one time period (1992-2001) using two generations of the National Land Cover Data (NLCD) (Vogelmann et al. 1998). The study found that 2.5% of the entire watershed experienced change, with forest and agriculture experiencing the largest declines in area (approximately2.3%). In addition, 49.3% of the changes were transitions from undeveloped to developed land with the greatest percentage of the overall watershed change occurring within 0-10 km of the shoreline (Wolter et al. 2006).

In northeastern Minnesota, White and Host (2003, 2008) used General Land Office (GLO) survey data and aerial photography from the 1930s, 1970s, and 1990s to quantify forest disturbance frequency and spatial patterns. They found an increase in fire frequency from pre-settlement (1860-1890) to the 1910-1940 period, followed by a decrease in fire frequency which was replaced by increases in timber harvest rates. A more recent study focused on forest cover type transitions and landscape structural changes in the same area using Landsat imagery from 1990-1995, found that of the mature forested area, 4.2% was harvested, flooded, or burned 5 years later (Wolter and White 2002). Not surprisingly, forest harvests were highest on private lands (ca. 1.7% per year) and lowest on tribal land (ca. 0.55% per year), with the greatest rates of disturbance of publicly managed land occurring on managed state forests (ca. 1.1% per year).

In a study that investigated the relationship and trends in land use and forest cover on private parcels in the upper Midwest from 1970 to 1990, developed land area increased in all counties in the study area. In addition, the percentage of land in agriculture declined between the 1980s and 1990s, but held steady in some counties when observed over the entire time period (1970s to 1990s) (Brown 2003). This could reflect the conversion of previously-cleared forest lands for agriculture, back to a forested cover type. However, this trend will likely not continue, since development continues to expand.

While all of the previously mentioned studies have provided useful information regarding land cover and land use, their geographic scope has been quite large and none of them has included any data regarding changes in Ontario, Canada. In addition, while there have been studies focused on beaver (Smith and Peterson 1988, Host and Meysembourg 2010), fire (Scheller et al. 2005), and blowdowns (Moser et al. 2007, Woodall and Nagel 2007), there has not been a study to incorporate multiple disturbance agents for VOYA and the adjacent areas. We are confident that this report will help fill this gap in the research literature and provides useful information to park resource managers.

Methods

Study Area

This study was conducted in one Landsat scene (path 27 row 26) in north central Minnesota and south central Ontario, Canada, around Voyageurs National Park (VOYA) (Figure 1). The area is a forest dominated landscape on the southern edge of boreal forest extent (Faber-Langendoen et al. 2007). The park covers 83,207 ha (205,609 acres), of which 65.3% is land, the rest open lakes and ponds (Table 1). The climate is mid-continental, with a mean annual temperature of 1.4 °C, annual extremes that may exceed -40 and 36 °C, and a mean annual precipitation of 630 mm (Kurmis et al. 1986). The landscape is dominated by Canadian Shield terrain, consisting of Early Precambrian granite, biotite schist, and migmatite. Centuries of erosion and glacial scouring during the Pleistocene have produced the current surficial geology features, which include sandy loam tills, lacustrine deposits, localized outwash deposits of sand and gravel, with bedrock often occurring within <0.1 m of the surface (Ojakangas and Matsch 1982).

The study area was divided into three different areas for summary and analysis purposes. The three areas were VOYA, Canada, and Minnesota (MN) (Figure 1). Outside the park, the analysis included an area ≥3 km from the border of the park; in Canada it was often nearly 6 km from the park boundary because of the large amount of water within 3 km of the park. The analysis area was based on a number of factors. To place VOYA in context to the surrounding areas, an analysis area which included adjacent lands to the park was needed. Common analysis areas used in research studies include watershed boundaries or a set buffer around the area of interest. Watershed boundaries are especially useful if the goal is to quantify inputs from the watershed, however, the watershed boundaries for VOYA were too large to analyze, due to limited staff resources. In addition, the goal of the project was not to quantify watershed characteristics. A set buffer works well in most cases, however the distance is often variable throughout studies and in landscape-scale studies is oftentimes limited by available resources. After multiple discussions with park resource staff, an analysis area was settled upon which balanced the factors previously mentioned. The analysis area was large enough to offer insight into adjacent land activities, while also being feasible from a operational perspective. Land and water areas of each of the analysis areas differ and have been summarized in Table 1. In total, ca. 150,000 hectares of land were analyzed, validated, and summarized for this summary report. For the remainder of the report the three analysis areas will be referred to as VOYA, MN, and Canada.

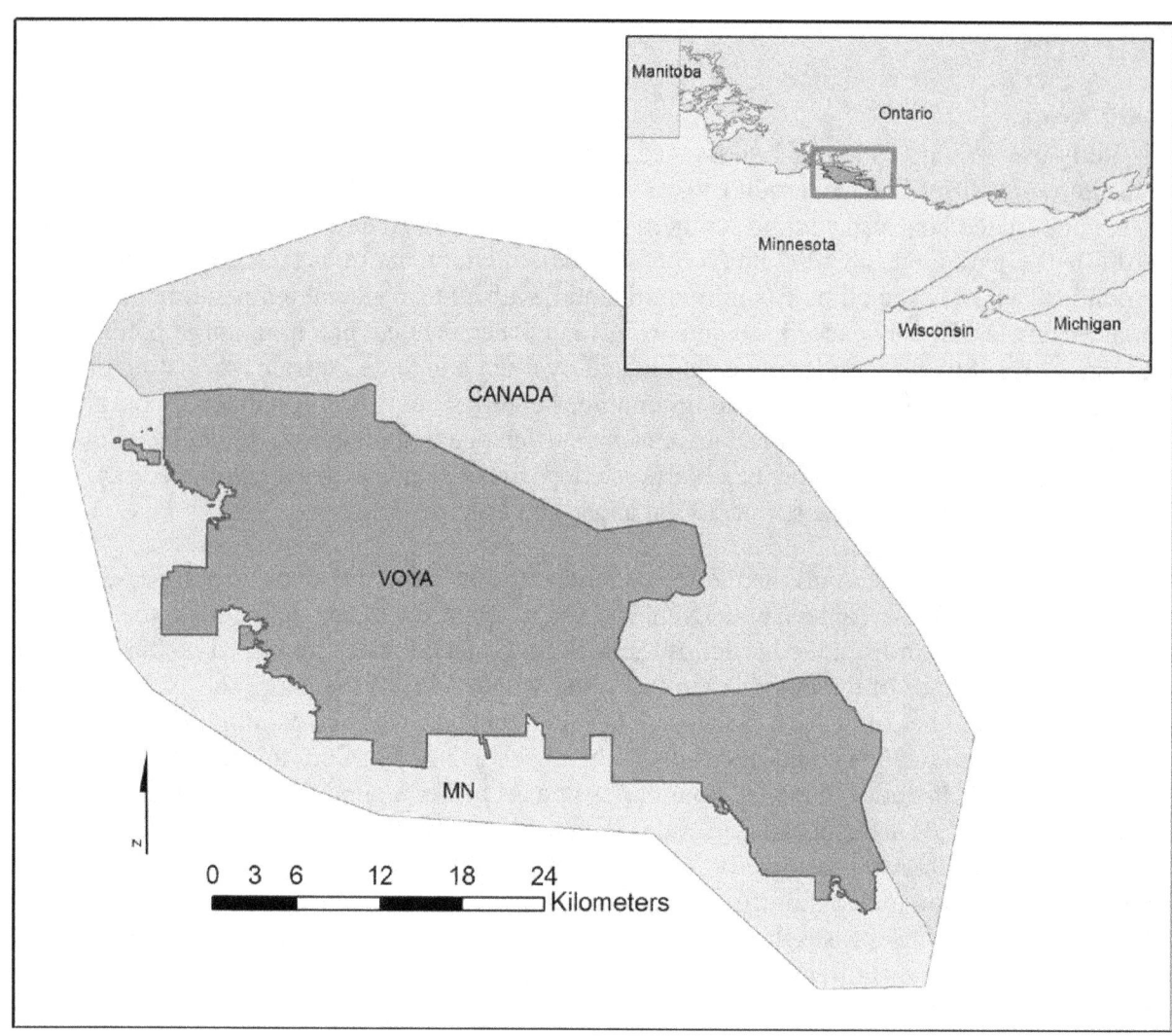

Figure 1. Study area for long-term monitoring of land cover in and adjacent to Voyageurs National Park. Green, light brown, and dark brown, indicate the park, a buffer in Minnesota, and a buffer in Canada, respectively.

Table 1. Areas (hectares) of each analysis region summarizing the total amount of land, water, and total area.

	Area specific					
	Land		Water		Total	
	Hectares	%	Hectares	%	Hectares	%[a]
VOYA	54,347	65	28,860	35	83,207	39
MN	37,761	85	6,506	15	44,267	20
Canada	55,765	63	32,816	37	88,581	41
Total	147,873	68	68,182	32	216,055	100

[a] = percent of grand total in the three areas.

Image Data and Processing

Landsat satellite imagery was downloaded from the Landsat data archive via the USGS's GLOVIS website (http://glovis.usgs.gov/). To minimize the effect of phenology, imagery was chosen for an approximately three month window (1 June – 31 August) during the peak of the growing season (Figure 3 and Table 2). For each year since 1984, the goal was to acquire enough imagery in the optimal phenological window such that one cloud-free composite of the entire analysis area could be used in the analysis. To aid in the production of the cloud-free composite, we also acquired a number of scan line corrector-off (SLC-off) images which include strips of no data as a result of the hardware malfunction (http://landsat.usgs.gov/products_slcoffbackground.php). In total, 56 images were downloaded and processed for analysis. After images were downloaded, we used the atmospheric correction described in Kennedy et. al (2007). For a single reference year, the COST correction is used to convert from Digital Counts to apparent surface reflectance. The COST correction includes a standard Dark Object Subtraction (DOS) correction to account for additive noise caused by aerosols, and then also includes a multiplicative correction using a first approximation of atmospheric transmission based on the cosine of the sun's zenith angle at the time of image acquisition (Chavez 1996).

The COST-corrected reference image is then used as the base for relative radiometric normalization of the remainder of the images in the stack. We used the Multiple Alteration Detection Calibration (MADCAL) automated approach for detection of stable targets, as evaluated by Schroeder et al. (2006), but applied to the special case of normalizing many images in a stack. Additional information regarding this technique can be found in Kennedy et al. (2010).

Finally, clouds and associated shadows were masked out by using an automated algorithm to calculate two continuous-variable scores, one for clouds and one shadows. The analyst manually determines the appropriate numerical threshold to separate cloud from non-cloud or cloud-shadow from non-cloud-shadow. These values are then used in an automated algorithm that develops binary masks for cloud and cloud shadow, combines them, and then adds a buffer to allow for cloud-edge effects on neighboring pixels.

Following image preprocessing, a number of computer algorithms, collectively known as "LandTrendr" were applied at the pixel (30 m x 30 m) level to identify disturbances. These disturbances are then grouped into similar patches and identified as individual polygons. Additional information regarding the LandTrendr process can be found in Kennedy et. al (2010), Kennedy et. al (2007), and Kennedy et. al (in review).

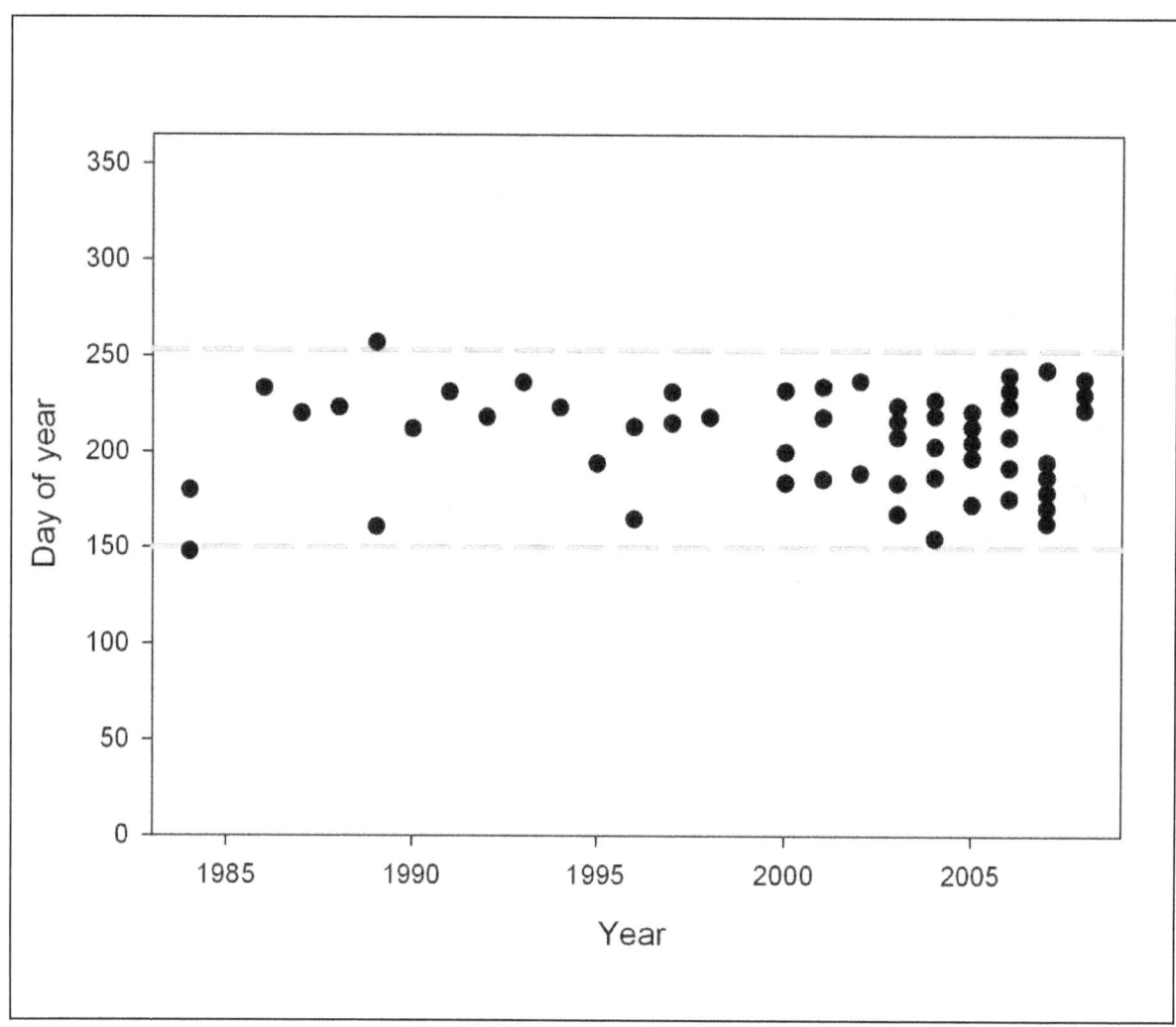

Figure 2. Day and year of 56 Landsat images used for analysis with green dotted lines denoting ideal phenological window between 1 June and 31 August.

Table 2. Dates and Landsat sensor for each of the 56 images acquired for path 27 row 26 and used for analysis of disturbances in and adjacent to VOYA.

Date	TM or ETM+[a]	Date	TM or ETM+[a]
5/27/1984	TM	7/27/2003	ETM+
6/28/1984	TM	8/4/2003	TM
8/21/1986	TM	8/12/2003	ETM+[b]
8/8/1987	TM	6/3/2004	TM
8/10/1988	TM	7/5/2004	TM
6/10/1989	TM	7/21/2004	TM
9/14/1989	TM	8/6/2004	TM
7/31/1990	TM	8/14/2004	TM
8/19/1991	TM	6/22/2005	TM
8/5/1992	TM	7/16/2005	ETM+[b]
8/24/1993	TM	7/24/2005	TM
8/11/1994	TM	8/1/2005	ETM+[b]
7/13/1995	TM	8/9/2005	TM
6/13/1996	TM	6/25/2006	TM
7/31/1996	TM	7/11/2006	TM
8/3/1997	TM	7/27/2006	TM
8/19/1997	TM	8/12/2006	TM
8/6/1998	TM	8/20/2006	ETM+[b]
7/2/2000	ETM+	8/28/2006	TM
7/18/2000	ETM+	6/12/2007	TM
8/19/2000	ETM+	6/20/2007	ETM+[b]
7/5/2001	ETM+	6/28/2007	TM
8/6/2001	ETM+	7/6/2007	ETM+[b]
8/22/2001	ETM+	7/14/2007	TM
7/8/2002	ETM+	8/31/2007	TM
8/25/2002	ETM+	8/9/2008	ETM+[b]
6/17/2003	TM	8/17/2008	TM
7/3/2003	TM	8/25/2008	ETM+[b]

[a] Thematic mapper (TM) or Enhance Thematic Mapper plus (ETM+) sensor
[b] denotes SLC-off image

Validation of Disturbances

After disturbance polygons were created, the next step was to validate whether a change actually occurred in the polygon. In addition to validating whether changes have occurred, additional information such as the change agent and starting/ending classes, were added during the validation process. Using high resolution imagery (Table 3), we were able to determine whether changes had indeed occurred and by using contextual information we were able to determine the disturbance agent. In addition to using high resolution imagery, we also employed the use of an OSU-developed application called TimeSync (Cohen et al. In review). This program allows the user to view composite image chips of the entire stack of Landsat imagery for pre-determined locations as well as the associated spectral trajectory of the pixel through time.

By viewing the high resolution aerial photos, temporally high resolution image chips, and spectral trajectories, the user was able to make a well-informed decision regarding the validity of the disturbance. To limit the potential for bias, the number of interpreters was limited to two, with one person validating all but one year of disturbances. To view the image chips and spectral trajectories, we used TimeSync, a program developed by researchers at Oregon State University (Cohen et al. In review). If a disturbance was validated within a polygon, additional attributes (fields) were populated within the feature class (Table 4) (Kirschbaum and Gafvert 2010a). To determine the starting class, or the most likely vegetation type that was disturbed, we used multiple land cover datasets, depending on best available data sources. In areas where the 1996 National Vegetation Classification System (NVCS) (Jennings et al. 2004) data was developed for VOYA using 1996 airphotos (Faber-Langendoen et al. 2007), we used this data as the basis for the starting class. In areas where the NVCS data was not available, we relied on the 2001 National Land-Cover Database (NLCD) (Homer et al. 2004) for MN and a 2000 land cover map for forested areas of Canada (Table 4) (Wulder et al. 2003).

Polygons were flagged for field visits when potential changes were detected, but could not be validated. Field visits were conducted in summer of 2008. There were a total of six polygons over the six years of disturbances that needed field validation. Field validation generally consisted of visiting the questionable polygons, while at the same time viewing LandTrendr outputs such as disturbance duration, year of disturbance, and disturbance magnitude. After examining the area on the ground, a qualitative decision was made regarding the type and cause of the disturbance (Kirschbaum and Gafvert 2010b).

Table 3. Aerial photos and high resolution satellite imagery used for validation.

Date	Resolution	Image spectrum	Contractor	Park coverage
7/1/1927	Unknown	B&W	Unknown	Partial
5/1/1992	1 m	B&W	APFO-NAPP	Complete
7/1/1995	1 m	CIR	MN DNR	Complete
7/1/1997	1 m	RGB	APFO-NAIP	Partial
7/1/2003	1 m	RGB	APFO-NAIP	Complete
8/1/2003	4 m	MS (4band)	IKONOS	Complete
10/1/2005	1 m	CIR	MN DNR	Complete
7/1/2006	1 m	RGB	APFO-NAIP	Partial
7/1/2007	10 m	MS (4band)	SPOT	Partial
5/24/2008	0.15 m	MS (4band)	Allied GIS/Pinnacle	Complete
5-8/1/2008	1 m	MS (4band)	APFO-NAIP	Complete

Table 4. Land cover datasets used for labeling the original land cover class for disturbed areas.

Analysis area	Dataset	Time period represented
Ontario, Canada	Earth Observation for Sustainable Development of Forests (EOSD)	2000
VOYA	National Vegetation Classification System	1996
Minnesota	National Land Cover Dataset	2001

Results

All results are reported in reference to land area, excluding water. Results for two very minor disturbance agent categories, insect/disease and unknown, were tracked but have been excluded from this report as they were insignificant across the three analysis areas (mean annual change <0.01% for both disturbances across all three areas).

Percent Land Disturbed

VOYA
During the six year period, a total of 0.68% of the land area inside the park was disturbed (Table 5). The year with the largest amount of disturbance was 2004 (0.26%), followed by 2002 and 2005 with 0.17 and 0.15% of land disturbed, respectively (Figure 3). The lowest years were 2003 and 2007, with 0.03% disturbed each year.

Canada
Collectively, 7.1% of the land area in the Canada analysis area was disturbed during the six year period (Table 5). In 2006, only 0.25% of the area was disturbed, in contrast to 2003 where 2.39% was disturbed (Figure 3).

MN
A total of 4.30% of the land was affected in the six year period for the MN analysis area (Table 5). Generally, the percent land disturbed in MN was stable through time, with a slight increase in 2003 (Figure 3).

Table 5. Percent of land disturbed by year and analysis area for the 6-year analysis period.

Year	% disturband land		
	VOYA	Canada	MN
2002	0.17	1.26	0.58
2003	0.03	2.39	1.22
2004	0.26	1.75	0.77
2005	0.15	0.97	0.80
2006	0.05	0.25	0.49
2007	0.03	0.48	0.44
Total	**0.68**	**7.10**	**4.30**

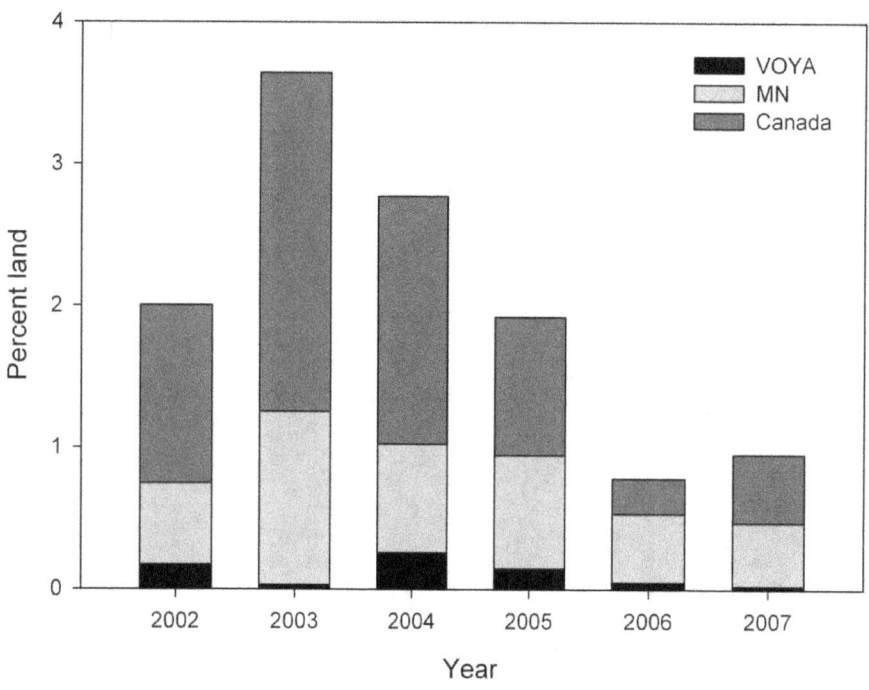

Figure 3. Percent of land disturbed by year and analysis area.

Disturbance Agents

VOYA

Inside the park, there were multiple disturbance agents present (Table 6). Fire affected the largest amount of land in the six year period, followed by beaver, and blowdown with 180, 95 and 82 hectares affected, respectively (Table 6). Flooding was the only other disturbance observed in the park, with only 2.9 hectares affected in the analysis period. No buildings (development) or forest harvest was detected inside the park during this time period. As a percent of the land in the analysis area, only 0.7% of the land in the park was disturbed in the six year period (Table 7). Of this, nearly half of the disturbed area occurred in 2004 with the Shoepack Lake fire (Figure 4a).

Canada

Forest harvest was the largest disturbance agent in the Canada analysis area, peaking in 2003 with >1300 ha harvested, and tapering down to ca. 200 ha harvested in 2007 (Figure 4b). In total nearly 4000 ha were harvested in the analysis period. The only other disturbance present in Canada were beaver and blowdown which, collectively, totaled ca. 80 ha (Table 6). As a percentage of the land present, nearly 7% of the land experienced forest harvest in the analyzed time period (Table 7). The remaining disturbance agents contributed <0.5% of the land affected (Figure 5c).

MN

In MN, there were four different disturbance agents detected. Forest harvest was the dominant disturbance agent on the landscape, with 1,559.3 ha harvested in the 6-year period (Table 6). Following forest harvest, blowdown, beaver, and building (development) were the remaining disturbance agents affecting 21.7, 23.1, and 17.7 ha, respectively. Beaver disturbance was

12

present in all but two years, with the largest amount occurring in 2007. Forest harvest was relatively stable through time, with 2003 experiencing the largest amount of land affected (Figure 4c). Small amounts of development occurred in 2005 and 2006, with the largest amount of development occurring in years 2003 and 2004 with 6.5 and 8.2 ha disturbed, respectively.

Table 6. Number and area (hectares) of disturbance events by disturbance agent and year for each analysis area.

| Analysis area | Year | No. events | Area disturbed (ha) by agent | | | | | | |
			Beaver	Blowdown	Building	Fire	Flooding	Forest harvest	Total
VOYA	2002	28	44.2	47.8	0.0	0.0	1.3	0.0	93.3
	2003	9	16.0	0.0	0.0	0.0	0.0	0.0	16
	2004	23	14.0	0.0	0.0	122.9	0.0	0.0	136.9
	2005	26	14.2	7.8	0.0	57.4	0.0	0.0	79.4
	2006	6	0.0	26.6	0.0	0.0	0.0	0.0	26.6
	2007	7	7.0	0.0	0.0	0.3	1.7	0.0	9
	Total	*99*	*95.4*	*82.2*	*0*	*180.6*	*3*	*0.0*	*361.2*
Canada	2002	38	40.2	26.1	0.0	0.0	0.0	593.2	659.5
	2003	39	11.1	0.0	0.0	0.0	0.0	1,306.6	1,317.7
	2004	23	3.2	0.0	0.0	0.0	0.0	971.8	975
	2005	32	3.1	0.0	0.0	0.0	0.0	539.6	542.7
	2006	3	0.0	0.0	0.0	0.0	0.0	136.9	136.9
	2007	36	0.0	0.0	0.0	0.0	0.0	199.3	199.3
	Total	*171*	*57.6*	*26.1*	*0.0*	*0.0*	*0.0*	*3,747.4*	*3,831.1*
MN	2002	30	5.1	21.7	1.8	0.0	0.0	189.1	217.7
	2003	47	0.0	0.0	6.5	0.0	0.0	454.7	461.2
	2004	42	4.9	0.0	8.2	0.0	0.0	277.0	290.1
	2005	29	0.9	0.0	0.4	0.0	0.0	300.7	302
	2006	26	0.0	0.0	0.8	0.0	0.0	182.8	183.6
	2007	27	12.2	0.0	0.0	0.0	0.0	155.0	167.2
	Total	*201*	*23.1*	*21.7*	*17.7*	*0.0*	*0.0*	*1,559.3*	*1,621.8*

Table 7. Percent of land disturbed by disturbance agent and year for each analysis area.

Analysis area	Year	Percent of land disturbed by agent						
		Beaver	Blowdown	Building	Fire	Flooding	Forest harvest	Total
VOYA	2002	0.08	0.09	0.00	0.00	<0.01	0.00	0.17
	2003	0.03	0.00	0.00	0.00	0.00	0.00	0.03
	2004	0.03	0.00	0.00	0.23	0.00	0.00	0.25
	2005	0.03	0.01	0.00	0.11	0.00	0.00	0.15
	2006	0.00	0.05	0.00	0.00	0.00	0.00	0.05
	2007	0.01	0.00	0.00	<0.01	<0.01	0.00	0.01
	Total	*0.18*	*0.15*	*0.00*	*0.33*	*0.01*	*0.00*	*0.67*
Canada	2002	0.07	0.05	0.00	0.00	0.00	1.06	1.18
	2003	0.02	0.00	0.00	0.00	0.00	2.34	2.36
	2004	0.01	0.00	0.00	0.00	0.00	1.74	1.75
	2005	0.01	0.00	0.00	0.00	0.00	0.97	0.97
	2006	0.00	0.00	0.00	0.00	0.00	0.25	0.25
	2007	0.00	0.00	0.00	0.00	0.00	0.36	0.36
	Total	*0.10*	*0.05*	*0.00*	*0.00*	*0.00*	*6.72*	*6.87*
MN	2002	0.01	0.06	<0.01	0.00	0.00	0.50	0.57
	2003	0.00	0.00	0.02	0.00	0.00	1.20	1.22
	2004	0.01	0.00	0.02	0.00	0.00	0.73	0.77
	2005	<0.01	0.00	<0.01	0.00	0.00	0.80	0.80
	2006	0.00	0.00	<0.01	0.00	0.00	0.48	0.48
	2007	0.03	0.00	0.00	0.00	0.00	0.41	0.44
	Total	*0.06*	*0.06*	*0.05*	*0.00*	*0.00*	*4.13*	*4.29*

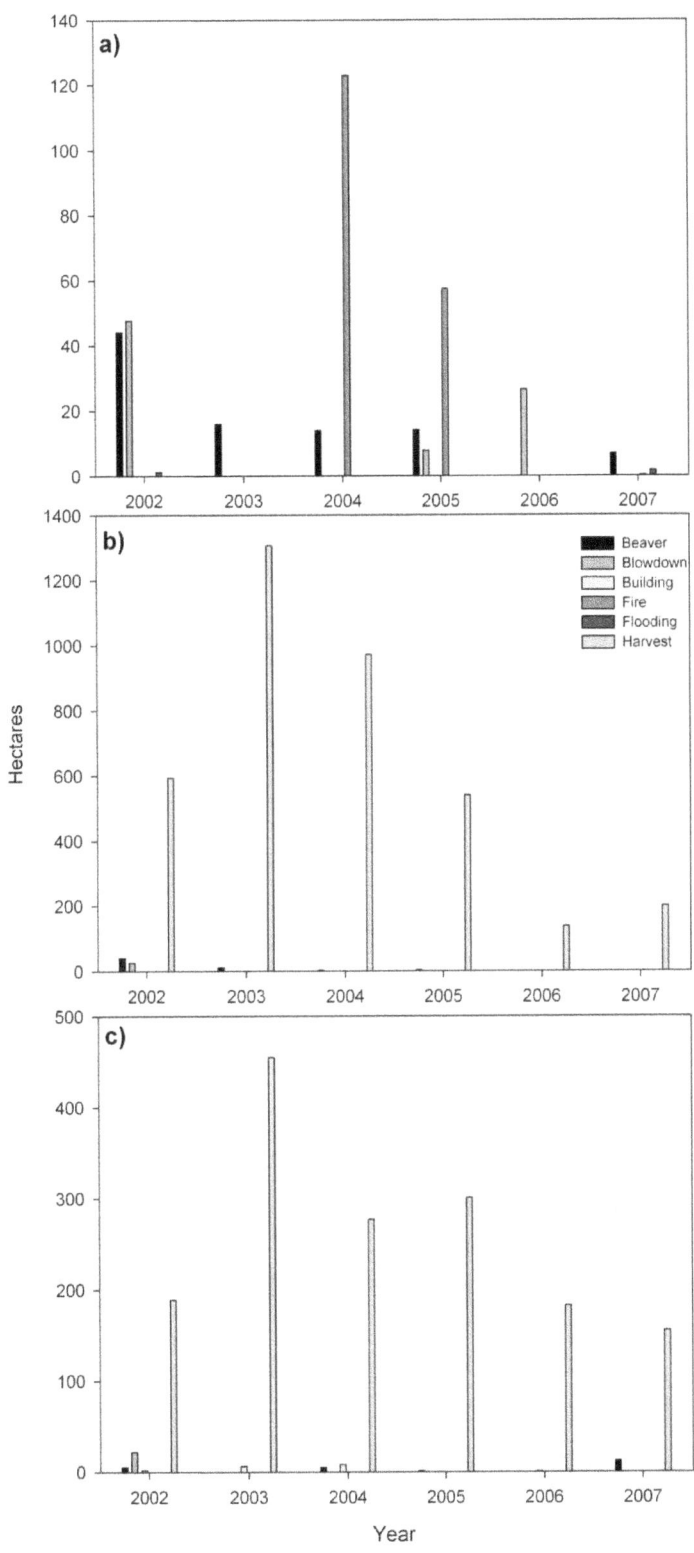

Figure 4. Hectares of land disturbed by disturbance agent and year for a) VOYA, b) Canada, and c) MN. Note differences in scale for each graph.

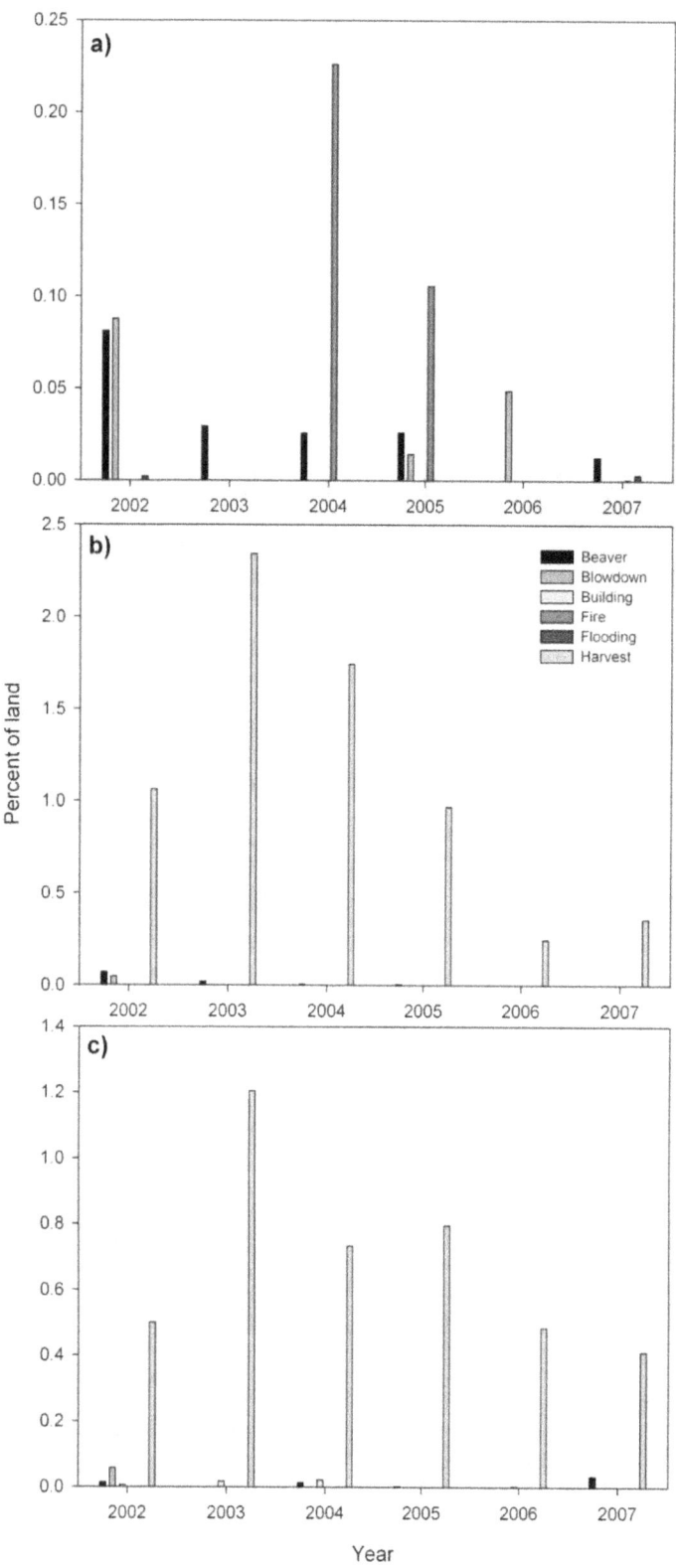

Figure 5. Percent of land affected by disturbance agent and year for a) VOYA, b) Canada, and c) MN. Note differences in scale for each area.

16

Disturbance Patches

VOYA

The most patches created by beaver occurred in 2002 (28), with no patches created in 2006 (Table 8). Years 2003, 2004, and 2005 had 9, 9, and 8 patches, respectively. The most patches due to blowdown events occurred in 2002 with 10 patches created on the landscape, and 2 and 6 patches in years 2005 and 2006, respectively. Patches created as a result of fire occurred in years 2004, 2005, and 2007, with 13, 16, and 1, respectively (Figure 6a). There were no patches created as a result of forest harvesting or building (development), and only two created from flooding. VOYA also had the smallest mean patch size (4.09 ha) among the analysis areas (Table 9 and Figure 7).

Canada

Forest harvesting created a total of 134 patches during the time period, with the largest number of patches occurring in 2003, with 36 (Table 8). The highest number of patches created from beaver activity occurred in 2002, with 9 patches, with all other years having ≤2 patches (Figure 6b). In 2002 there were 3 patches created as a result from blowdown, with no other blowdown patches for the remainder of the time period. There were also no building, fire, or flooding patches created in Canada (Table 8). Of the three analysis areas, Canada had the largest mean and maximum patch size at 23 ha and 396 ha, respectively (Table 9 and Figure 7).

MN

In MN, the number of patches created by forest harvest was relatively stable through time, with a total of 176 patches during the analysis period (Table 9). The maximum number of patches was created in 2003, with a total of 43 patches (Figure 8b). There were also 12 and 9 patches created by beaver and building (development), respectively, during the time period and no patches created as a result of fire or flooding (Table 8). The mean patch size in MN was ca. 8 ha, with a maximum patch size of ca. 74 ha (Table 9 and Figure 7).

Table 8. Number of disturbance patches by year and disturbance agent for each analysis area.

Analysis area	Year	Number of disturbance patches by agent						
		Beaver	Blowdown	Building	Fire	Flooding	Forest harvest	Total
VOYA	2002	17	10	0	0	1	0	28
	2003	9	0	0	0	0	0	9
	2004	9	0	0	13	0	0	22
	2005	8	2	0	16	0	0	26
	2006	0	6	0	0	0	0	6
	2007	3	0	0	1	1	0	5
	Total	*46*	*18*	*0*	*30*	*2*	*0*	*96*
Canada	2002	9	3	0	0	0	25	37
	2003	1	0	0	0	0	36	37
	2004	1	0	0	0	0	22	23
	2005	2	0	0	0	0	29	31
	2006	0	0	0	0	0	2	2
	2007	0	0	0	0	0	20	20
	Total	*13*	*3*	*0*	*0*	*0*	*134*	*150*
MN	2002	4	3	1	0	0	22	30
	2003	0	0	4	0	0	43	47
	2004	4	0	2	0	0	36	42
	2005	1	0	1	0	0	27	29
	2006	0	0	1	0	0	25	26
	2007	3	0	0	0	0	23	26
	Total	*12*	*3*	*9*	*0*	*0*	*176*	*200*

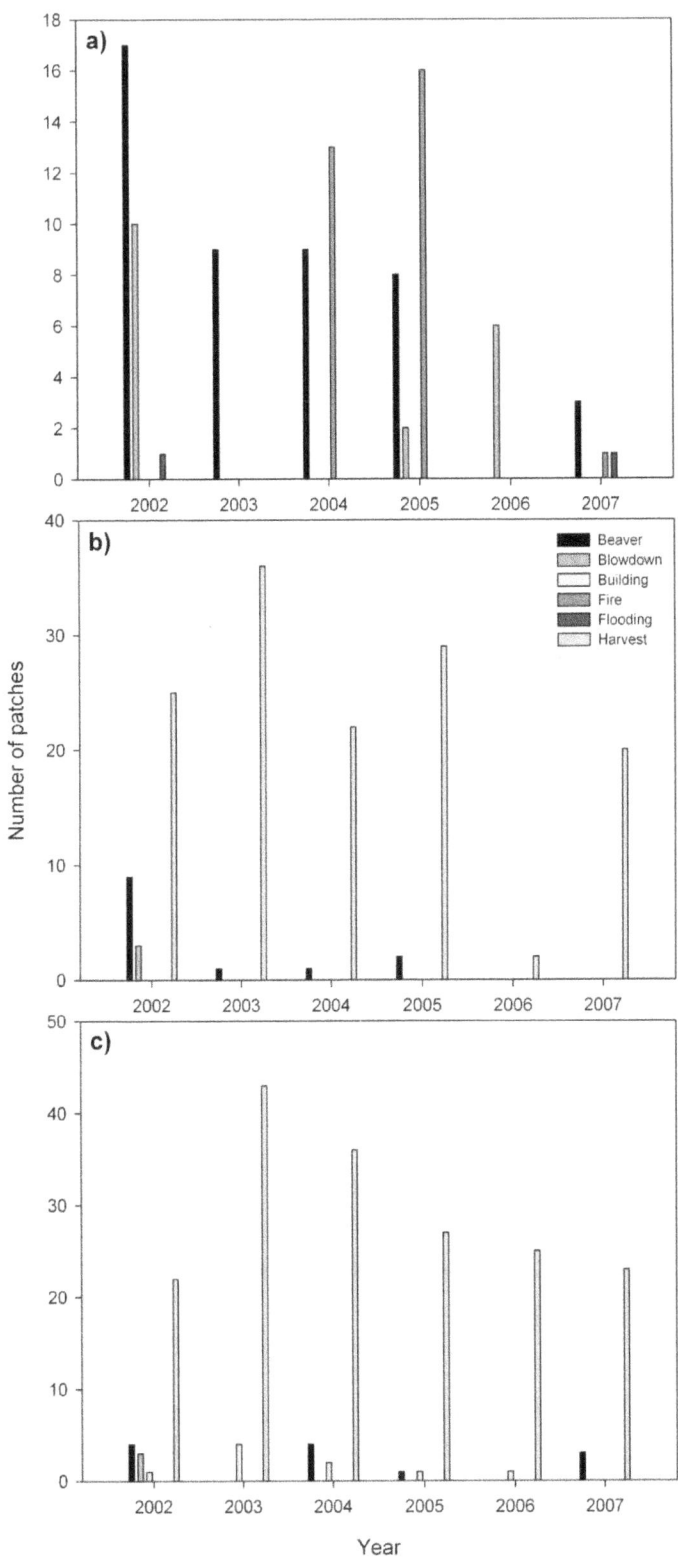

Figure 6. Number of patches by year and disturbance agent for a) VOYA, b) Canada, and c) MN. Note differences in scale for each area.

Table 9. The count, mean, minimum, maximum, and median size (ha) of disturbance patches for the three analysis areas.

Analysis area	Count	Patch size (ha)			
		Mean	*Minimum*	*Maximum*	*Median*
VOYA	96	4.09	0.19	64.08	1.76
Canada	150	23.15	0.79	396.27	6.12
MN	200	8.07	0.32	73.94	3.60

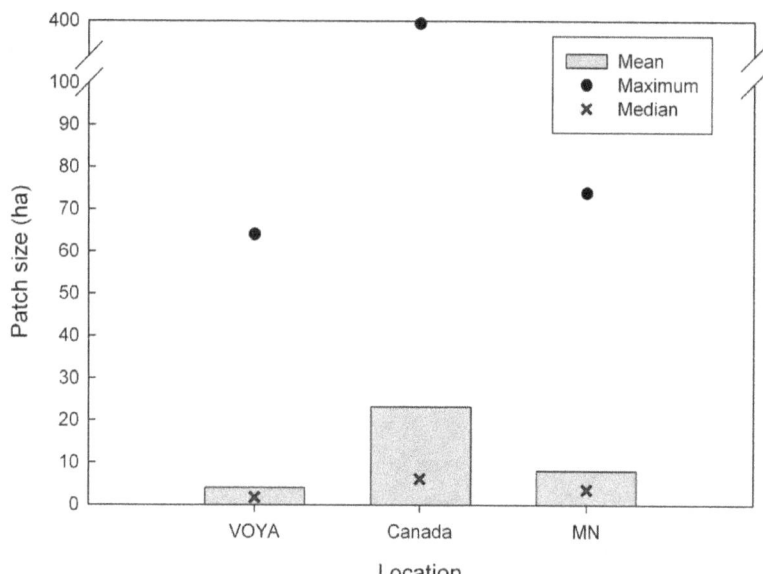

Figure 7. Mean, maximum, and median patch size (ha) for the three analysis areas.

Land Cover Dynamics

VOYA

In the park, some of each pre-disturbance cover type was converted during the analysis period, with upland forest being the largest cover type converted, totaling 187.6 ha. The three years with the most upland forest conversion were 2004-2006 (Figure 8a). Water and upland woodland were the next two largest conversion types with 62.4 and 45.5 ha converted, respectively (Table 10). Most of the water conversion occurred in 2002 (43.3 ha), in addition to years 2003-2005 (Figure 9a). There were additional small amounts of upland shrub/herbaceous and lowland shrub/herbaceous conversion with 1.5 and 6.5 ha converted, respectively in the analysis period.

Most upland forest transitioned to upland shrub/herbaceous, with water converting to lowland shrub/herbaceous (Figure 9a and Table 11). In addition, some water was added in all years except 2003 and 2006. There was no upland woodland or lowland forest added during the analysis period (Table 11).

Canada

Upland forest comprised the vast majority of cover type conversion in Canada (Figure 8b). A total of 3781 ha of upland forest was converted, largely because of forest harvesting. Some upland shrub/herbaceous was converted as well, totaling 139.3 ha during this time period (Table 10). There was no upland woodland or lowland forest converted and a small amount (12 ha) of lowland shrub/herbaceous.

The vast majority of upland forest was converted to upland shrub/herbaceous, totaling 3817.5 ha (Table 11 and Figure 9b). The only other two cover types which resulted from disturbances were lowland shrub/herbaceous, with 74.6 and 4.2 ha gained, respectively (Table 11).

MN

Minnesota experienced cover type conversions similar to that of Canada, with the majority of conversion occurring in upland forests, totaling 1,320 ha in the time period (Table 10 and Figure 8c). Year 2003 experienced the highest amount of upland forest conversion, with 371 ha being converted. Remaining cover types which were converted included upland woodland, lowland forest, and water, totaling 62.2, 19.3, and 16.6 ha, respectively. Upland and lowland shrub/herbaceous classes experienced no changes during the time period.

Similar to Canada, MN upland forest was largely converted to upland shrub/herbaceous (Table 11 and Figure 9c). There was also a significant amount of lowland shrub/herbaceous added, totaling 238.4 ha in the time period. Years 2002 and 2003 experienced the majority of these conversions, with some lowland shrub/herbaceous added each year of the time period. There was no upland forest, upland woodland, lowland forest cover types added, and a small amount (1.7 ha) of water added during the time period (Table 11).

Table 10. Area converted (ha) by year and cover type for three analysis areas.

Analysis area	Year	Area converted (ha), by cover type					
		Upland forest	Upland woodland	Upland shrub/ herbaceous	Lowland forest	Lowland shrub/ herbaceous	Water
VOYA	2002	18.7	0	0	3.5	0	43.3
	2003	3.3	0	0	1.8	2.3	1.4
	2004	79.7	37.6	0	3.9	2.9	5.5
	2005	53.9	7.9	1.5	0	1.3	12.2
	2006	26.5	0	0	0	0	0
	2007	5.5	0	0	1.7	0	0
	Total	*187.6*	*45.5*	*1.5*	*10.9*	*6.5*	*62.4*
Canada	2002	622.3	0	40.3	0	0	37.2
	2003	1,306.6	0	27.6	0	11.0	0
	2004	974.9	0	0	0	0	0
	2005	540.4	0	1.0	0	1.0	1.9
	2006	137.6	0	0	0	0	0
	2007	199.3	0	70.4	0	0	0
	Total	*3,781.1*	*0*	*139.3*	*0*	*12*	*39.1*
MN	2002	147.2	0	0	3.6	0	2.3
	2003	371.0	4.7	0	6.1	0	0
	2004	273.3	11.9	0	1.7	0	2.1
	2005	236.9	45.6	0	5.1	0	0
	2006	164.1	0	0	0	0	0
	2007	127.5	0	0	2.8	0	12.2
	Total	*1,320*	*62.2*	*0*	*19.3*	*0*	*16.6*

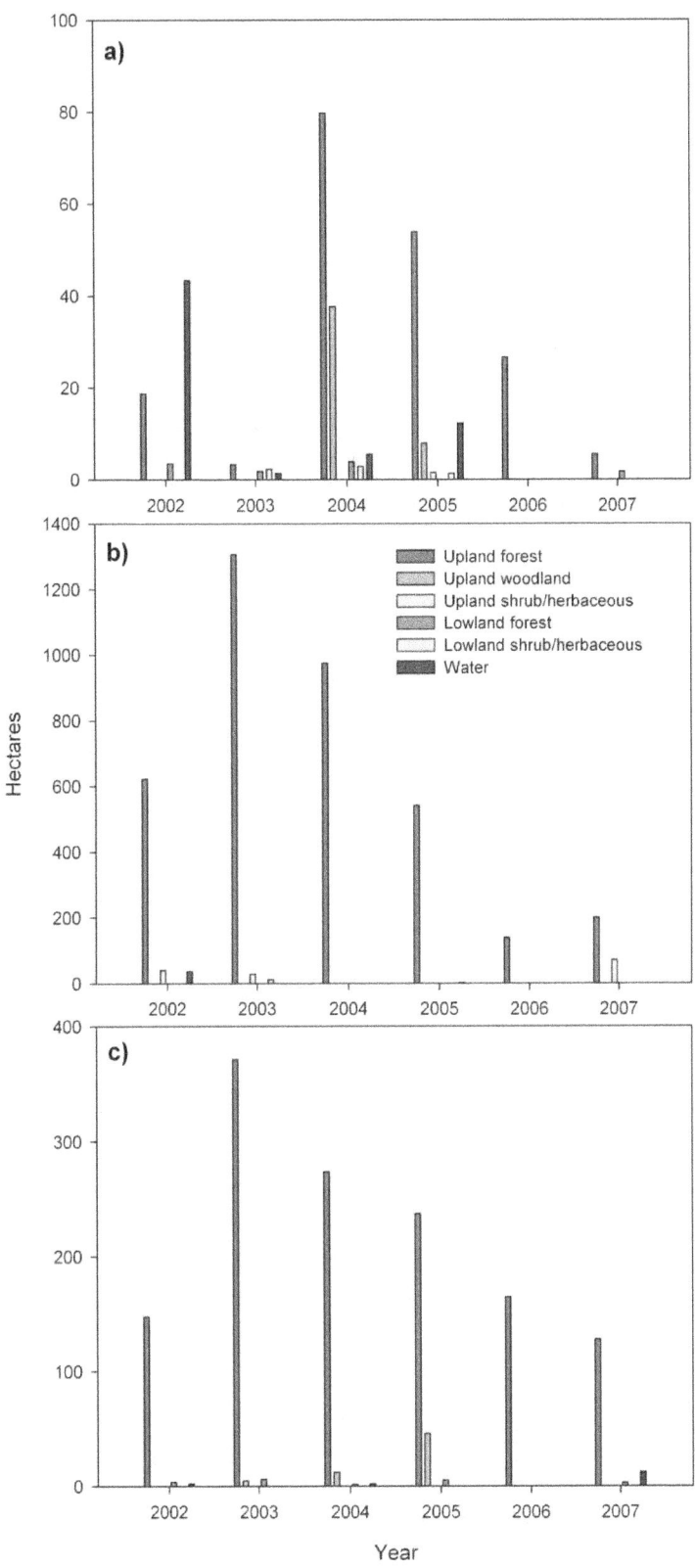

Figure 8. Area of cover types lost by year in a) VOYA, b) Canada, and c) MN

Table 11. Area gained (ha) in each cover type due to disturbances for the three analysis areas.

Analysis area	Year	Area gained (ha), by cover type					
		Upland forest	Upland woodland	Upland shrub / herbaceous	Lowland forest	Lowland shrub / herbaceous	Water
VOYA	2002	0.0	0.0	18.7	0.0	73.8	0.7
	2003	0.0	0.0	3.4	0.0	12.6	0.0
	2004	2.3	0.0	112.2	0.0	18.4	3.5
	2005	0.0	0.0	58.2	0.0	15.2	1.1
	2006	0.0	0.0	26.6	0.0	0.0	0.0
	2007	4.7	0.0	0.3	0.0	6.5	2.2
	Total	*7.0*	*0.0*	*219.3*	*0.0*	*126.5*	*7.5*
Canada	2002	0.0	0.0	663.6	0.0	37.2	0.0
	2003	0.0	0.0	1,318.7	0.0	21.8	0.0
	2004	0.0	0.0	918.6	0.0	0.0	3.2
	2005	0.0	0.0	530.7	0.0	15.6	1.1
	2006	0.0	0.0	137.7	0.0	0.0	0.0
	2007	0.0	0.0	248.2	0.0	0.0	0.0
	Total	*0.0*	*0.0*	*3,817.5*	*0.0*	*74.6*	*4.2*
MN	2002	0.0	0.0	216.4	0.0	70.2	0.5
	2003	0.0	0.0	464.5	0.0	85.3	0.0
	2004	0.0	0.0	282.0	0.0	4.8	0.4
	2005	0.0	0.0	300.7	0.0	18.4	0.9
	2006	0.0	0.0	182.8	0.0	19.5	0.0
	2007	0.0	0.0	165.5	0.0	40.3	0.0
	Total	*0.0*	*0.0*	*1,611.9*	*0.0*	*238.4*	*1.7*

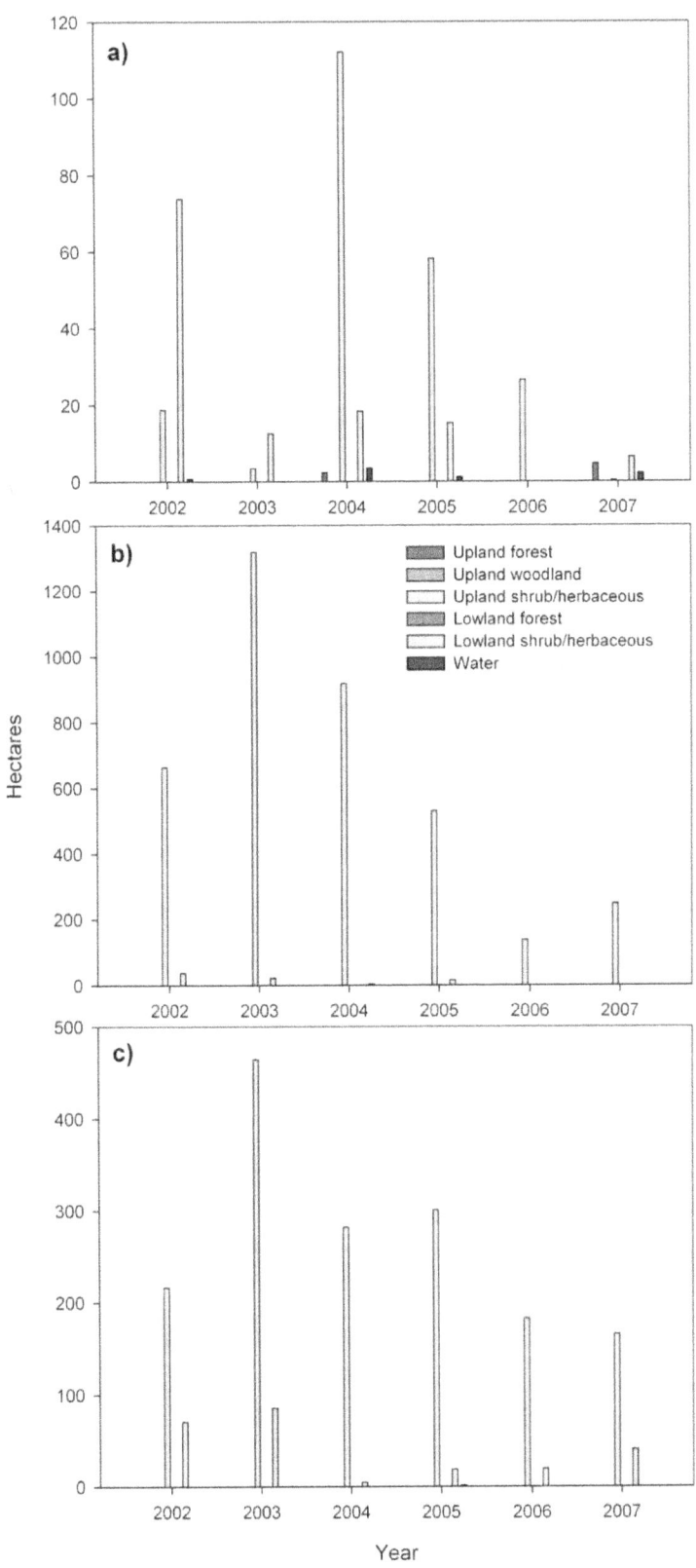

Figure 9. Area of cover types gained by year in a) VOYA, b) Canada, and c) MN.

Discussion

Voyageurs

Disturbance agents

Multiple natural disturbance agents were present inside the park during the six year period. Disturbances caused by beaver were the most consistent agent through time, with only one year (2006) in which no disturbances were attributed to beaver (Figure 6a). Beaver have been a dominant disturbance agent in the park for many years, with historical and current studies being carried out to track their health and overall population (Smith and Peterson 1988, Host and Meysembourg 2010). Populations have fluctuated through time with some of the fluctuation due to changes in suitable habitat as a result of rule curve (water level management) changes on Rainy Lake and the Namakan Reservoir (Smith and Peterson 1988, Johnston and Naiman 1990, S. Windels unpublished data). Our data shows that the area disturbed by beaver has been relatively stable since 2003. However, in 2006 and 2007, there were zero and three patches attributed to beaver disturbances, respectively (Table 8). The number and total area of disturbance caused by beaver declined over the six year period (Table 6, Figure 4a). Although this decline is not statistically significant, it likely reflects an overall decline in beaver abundance in the park as the area transitions to more climax forest. When LandTrendr is run at VOYA again in 2015, we will have a longer-term dataset to make further inferences.

Fire disturbed the largest area of land during the six year window (Table 6). In this time period there were two distinct fires which occurred inside the park. A naturally ignited fire (lightning) occurred in 2004 near Shoepack Lake, and was allowed to burn naturally (pers. comm., S. Windels, Voyageurs National Park, 2010). The results from LandTrendr showed that the fire affected approximately 120 ha in 2004, and about 60 ha the following year. This lag effect is most likely a result of trees being stressed and weakened by the 2004 fire, resulting in mortality the following year. The spatial component of this data also reveals that the fire did not create a single large scar, but rather a combination of open patches intermixed with numerous patches of forest that survived, providing a mosaic of habitats and seed source throughout the area for revegetation (Figure 10). Further, a total of only ca. 180 ha experienced change as detected by LandTrendr within the entire 576 ha of area burned, as mapped by technicians on the ground (Figure 10). In addition to the Shoepack Lake fire, there was a prescribed burn in 2008 which resulted in a small amount of tree mortality. In the next run of LandTrendr, we may find additional mortality from fire-stressed trees. Fire has historically been an important element of this southern boreal ecosystem, with fire return intervals ranging from 3-350 years depending on the cover type and intensity level (Heinselman 1973, 1996; Scheller et al. 2005; White and Host 2008). Allowing naturally occurring fires to burn and the continued use of prescribed fires will assist in maintaining this historically important component of the landscape.

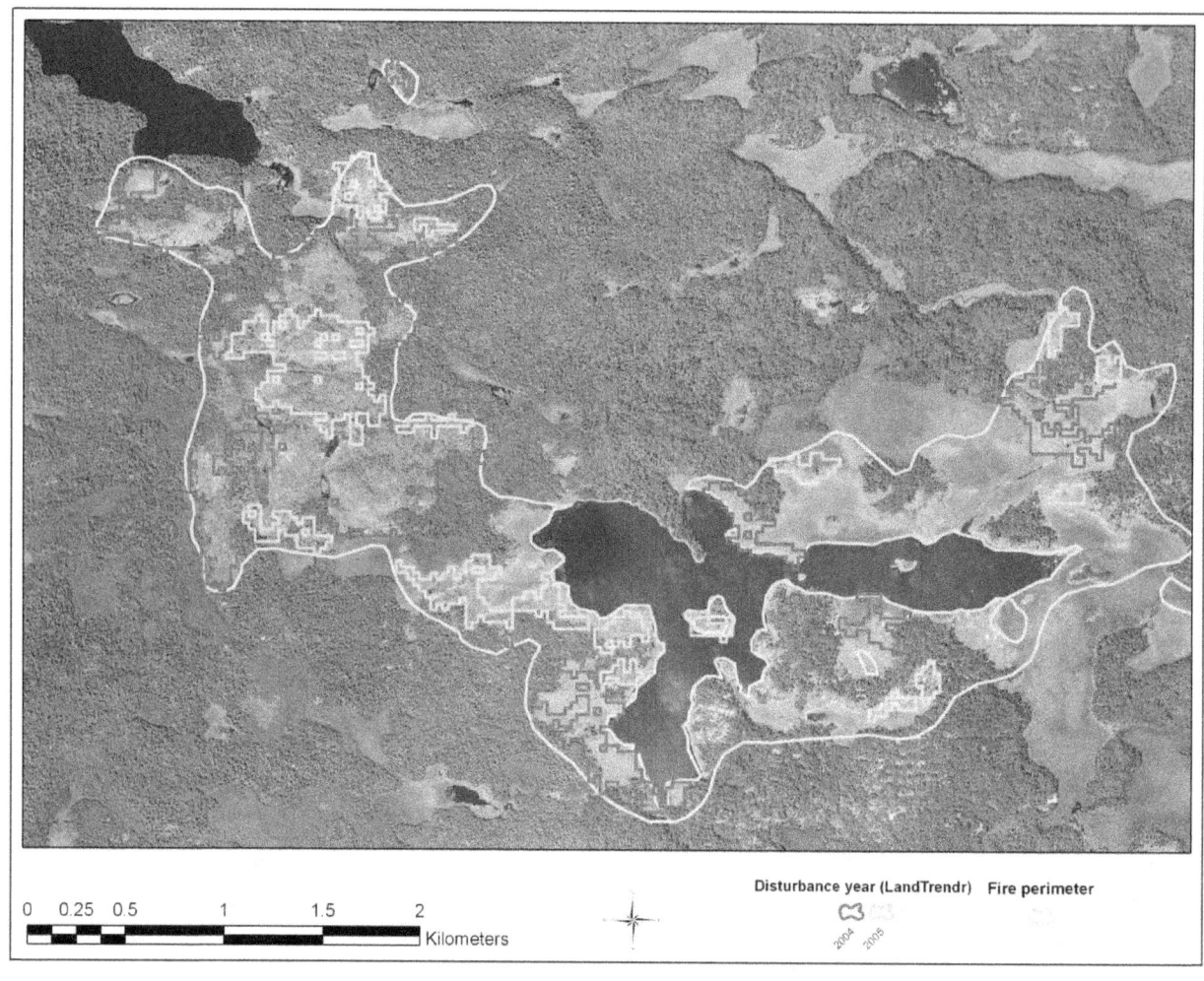

Figure 10. Example of mosaic pattern of 2004 Shoepack Lake fire showing tree mortality occurring in 2004 (red outline) and 2005 (green outline) and the fire perimeter as delineated by crews on the ground (light blue outline).

Land cover dynamics

Disturbances inside the park occurred in upland and lowland forest, upland woodland, upland and lowland shrub/herbaceous, and water. Upland forest had the largest amount of area lost, mainly in 2004 and 2005 due to the Shoepack fire. Also of note was an area in the water class which was lost in 2002 when Shoepack Lake experienced a breach in a beaver dam which had kept the lake at higher levels. This disturbance exposed >40 ha of lowland herbaceous land. In the future beaver may rebuild the dam at Shoepack Lake and re-flood the lowland herbaceous land. In the interim, these newly exposed areas could change from herbaceous to shrub, and eventually lowland forest, if conditions allow.

As a result of the disturbances occurring in the six year window, nearly all of the areas were converted to either upland or lowland shrub/herbaceous (Figure 9a). Since nearly all of the disturbances detected were stand replacing (total canopy removal), this is not uncommon for these disturbed areas. If left undisturbed these areas will likely follow a trajectory back to closed canopy forest conditions (Frelich and Reich 1995, Frelich 2002). The conversion of upland forest to upland shrub/herbaceous provides unique patches of young grass, shrubs, and tree seedlings for multiple types of wildlife. In addition, the pattern of land cover created by the Shoepack fire is a good example of the resulting complex mosaic resulting from natural disturbance processes.

Canada

Disturbance agents

The dominant disturbance agent in the Canada analysis area is forest harvest, which dwarfs any other disturbance agent. This is not uncommon in the heavily-managed forest lands of southern Ontario. These lands are dominated by private industrial management, and the large Boise Cascade paper mill located in International Falls, MN, and Fort Frances, Ontario, which drives the high demand for wood fiber in the region. During the analysis period, 7.1% of the land was harvested, or 1.18% per year. This is slightly higher rate than the 0.82% found by Walter and White (2002) during their analysis in northeastern MN from 1990-1995. If this trend continues, all land area in the Canada analysis area will be harvested in approximately 84 years. While this rotation cycle may seem feasible, this incorporates all land area, not accounting for areas that could not support merchantable timber. These harvested areas average 25 ha in size, with some larger forest harvests also occurring (Figure 7). From interpreting the available imagery, it appears that harvests typically remove all overstory trees. We are not able to determine from this analysis if it is whole tree harvest or if stems are the only part of the trees being removed. However, clearcutting with little residual basal area is very common for Ontario with the entire tree often chipped on site for wood fiber (pers. comm., S. Windels, Voyageurs National Park, 2010). The addition of a new biomass burner in Fort Frances will likely increase the demand for biomass which in turn affects the amounts of biomass (carbon) removed from the forest, impacting the overall carbon cycle and long-term sustainability of the forest (Johnson 1992, Nabuurs et al. 1997, Johnson and Curtis 2001, White et al. 2005).

The lack of fire disturbances is something to monitor in the future. Since this landscape is heavily managed, the lack of stand-replacing fires is not surprising, but should be noted because of the niche habitats created by a fire, for both animals and vegetation (Rowe and Scotter 1973, Koehler and Hornocker 1977, Lyon et al. 2000, Heyerdahl et al. 2001, Scheller et al. 2005). We will continue to monitor for fire disturbances into the future and may see an increase in forest fires if current drought conditions persist in the area. The National Oceanic and Atmospheric Administration (NOAA) reports that northern MN and southern Ontario are currently experiencing severe to moderate drought conditions (LeComte 2010), and the National Interagency Fire Center predicts above normal fire potential for the region (National Interagency Coordination Center Predictive Services 2010).

The lack of disturbances caused by beavers could be due the relatively little, and in some cases no, high resolution imagery available for validation. If LandTrendr did delineate new disturbances caused by beaver, especially small (1-2 ha) disturbances, we could have classified it as a 'false' disturbance due to the lack of high resolution imagery. However, in some cases where the beaver disturbance was large and distinct, by using the Landsat imagery and spectral trajectories, we were able to validate a beaver disturbance. In the case of severe wind events resulting in downed trees, there is a possibility that these were attributed to harvests, especially if the trees were salvaged shortly after the event, leaving no evidence of downed trees in the available high resolution imagery. The shape of these disturbances, and presence of roads to these openings further suggests it was harvest rather than blowdown.

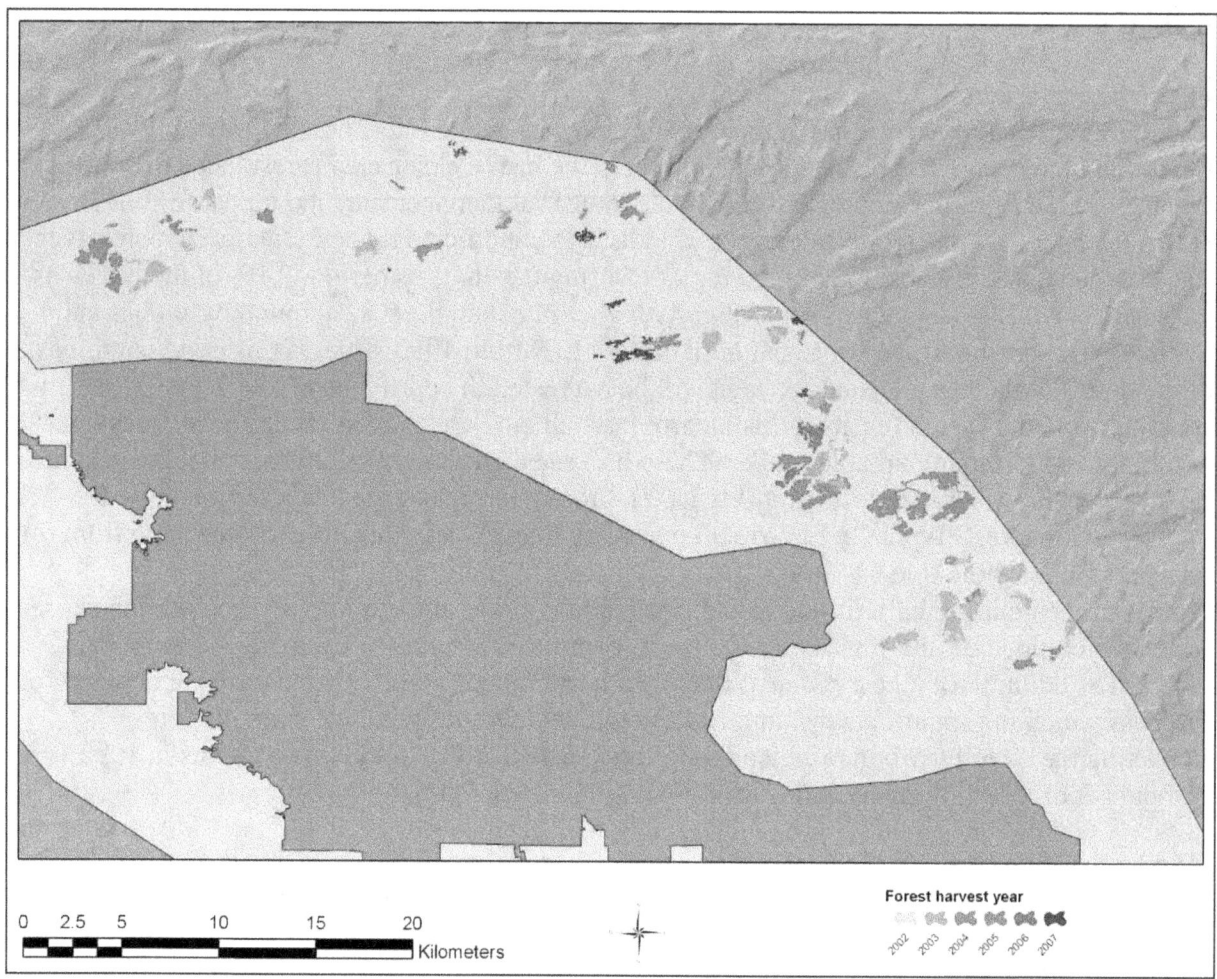

Figure 11. Forest harvest patches in Canada for the analysis time period with the three analysis areas in beige (MN), green (VOYA), and gray (Canada).

Land cover dynamics

Based upon the land cover dataset used (Table 5), 95% of the disturbed cover types started as upland forest and was converted to upland shrub/herbaceous. The remaining 5% of cover types disturbed included upland shrub/herbaceous, lowland shrub/herbaceous and water. Due to the fact that most of the disturbances were caused by forest harvesting, it coincides with the loss of upland forest land.

Assuming that regeneration (artificial and/or natural) and succession occur, we could expect these harvested areas to progress into a mixed forest type (Frelich and Reich 1995, Frelich 2002). In the meantime, these harvested areas are assumed to be in the upland herbaceous/shrub cover type. Depending on market demands and current management strategies, some of these areas could be planted back to a spruce/fir forest, or more mixed forest types.

Minnesota

Disturbance agents

As in Canada, the largest proportion of the land disturbed was attributed to forest harvest (Figure 5c and Table 7). Nearly one-third of land monitored in MN was under management of the Superior National Forest, with the remaining land being owned by county, state, and private individuals (Figure 12). On average, 0.68% of the land was harvested per year, which was relatively constant through the 6 years, except for 2003 when about 1.2% of the land was harvested. Forest harvests at this rate result in a ca. 145 year rotation, which is approximately twice that of Canada. This harvest rate is slightly lower than the 0.84% per year found by Wolter and White (2002). Multiple reasons exist for this disparity, including ownership patterns, timber demand, and stumpage prices.

Remaining disturbance agents included blowdown, beaver, and development. However, combined, these represented less than 5% of the total area disturbed. While these disturbances are not significant in terms of amount of landscape affected, it is important that development (building) remained quite low (Figure 7c). Since this area is desirable in terms of recreational opportunities, this will be an important metric to monitor in the future (McGranahan 1999, Brown 2003, Hammer et al. 2004). Gimmi et al. (2009) found that the establishment of National Parks at Indiana Dunes and Pictured Rocks National Lakeshores was likely responsible for the enhanced development and landscape fragmentation after park establishment. However, given the large distance from population centers and rising fuel prices, VOYA may not experience adjacent development as quickly as parks closer to urban areas. It will be important to note not only the amount, but spatial patterns and what cover types are being converted for development. In the interim, we will continue to monitor disturbances as a result of development which meet or exceed our minimum mapping unit (mmu) of 1 ha.

Land cover dynamics

Due to the large amount of forest harvests, upland forest comprised the majority of land cover conversion. In addition to upland forest, upland woodland, lowland forest, and water were also converted, but to a lesser degree (Table 11 and Figure 10c). Some of these conversions were a result of beaver activity or development which had occurred during the analysis period.

Nearly all of the disturbances were converted to either upland or lowland shrub/herbaceous cover types (Table 11 and Figure 9c). There was some area converted to water but this totaled only 1.7 ha during the analysis period. Due to the nature of the dominant disturbance agent, forest harvest, this conversion is expected.

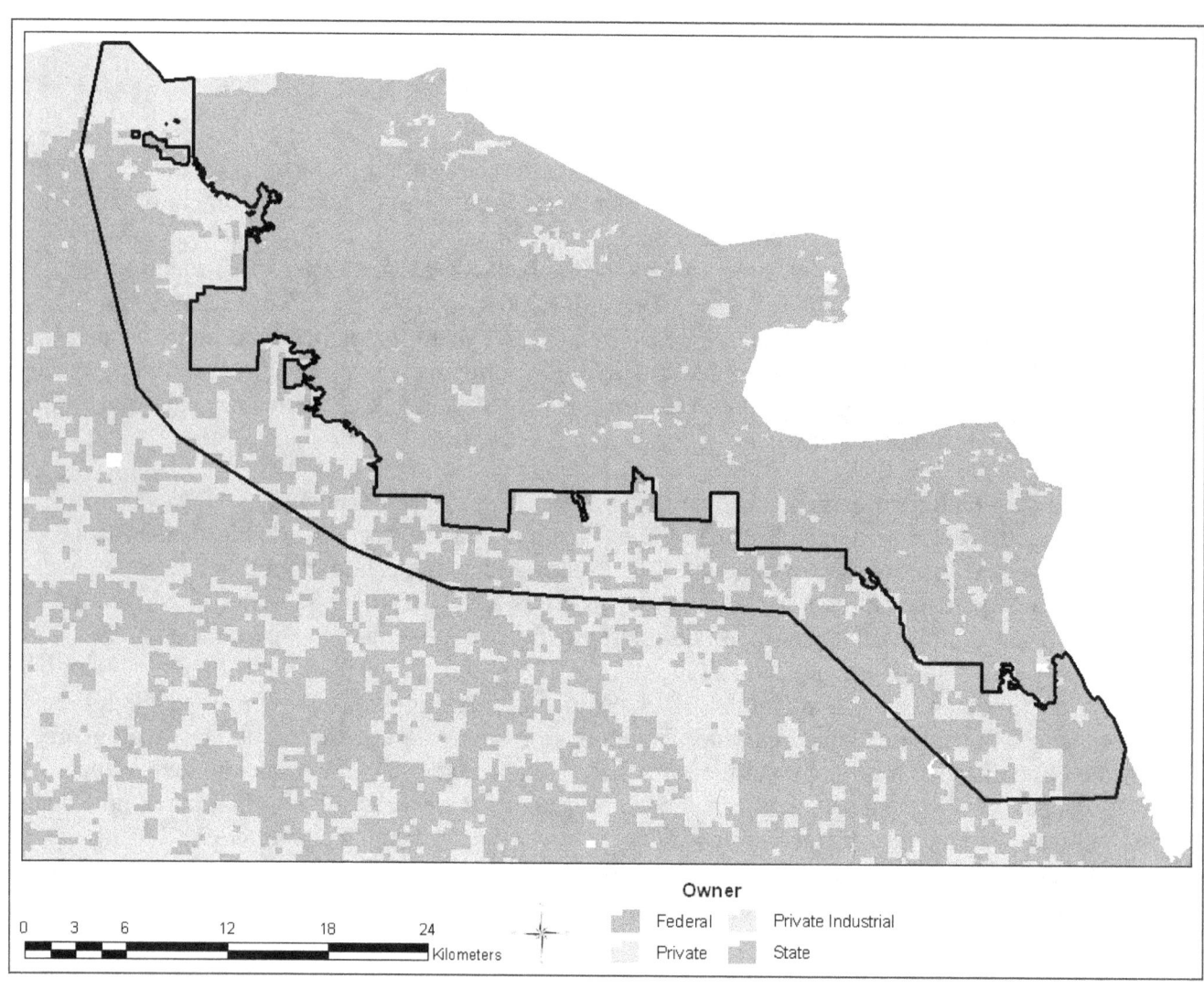

Figure 12. Land ownership in the MN analysis area (solid black line). Ownership data from the MN GAP analysis program (http://deli.dnr.state.mn.us/metadata.html?id=L390005860201).

Conclusions

The results clearly show far less disturbance occurring within the park compared with the adjacent landscape in Canada and Minnesota. The predominant disturbance agent outside the park is forest harvest, whereas the prohibition on logging within the park boundary reveals more 'natural' disturbance dynamics, driven predominantly by strong winds (and subsequent blowdown), fire, and beaver activity. Fire is also more represented inside the park than the surrounding area, an important distinction creating a more unique fragmented landscape promoting fire-dependent pine species.

The relatively large size and contiguous forest of Voyageurs National Park provides an opportunity for these natural disturbance agents to function nearly as they occurred prior to European settlement and subsequent influence on land cover. Large-scale fires or blowdowns will affect the composition and pattern of plant communities, but not threaten the forest matrix. The forest within the park boundary is still relatively young, as virtually all of the area was logged between 1900-1970 (Faber-Langendoen et al. 2007). Natural succession is now replacing much of the early aspen/birch stands to mixed hardwood and conifer (Frelich and Reich 1995). This natural progression is likely resulting in lower beaver numbers due to their preference for aspen for winter food. We would expect disturbance by beaver to continue as an important factor with increases and declines associated with changes in lowland forest.

Literature Cited

Brown, D. G. 2003. Land use and forest cover on private parcels in the upper Midwest USA, 1970 to 1990. Landscape Ecology 18:777-790.

Chavez, P. S. 1996. Image-based atmospheric corrections revisited and improved. Photogrammetric Engineering and Remote Sensing 62:1025-1036.

Cohen, W. B., Z. Yang, and R. E. Kennedy. In review. Detecting trends in forest disturbance and recovery using yearly Landsat time series: 2. TimeSync - Tools for calibration and validation. Remote Sensing of Environment.

Faber-Langendoen, D., N. Aaseng, K. Hop, M. Lew-Smith, and J. Drake. 2007. Vegetation classification, mapping, and monitoring at Voyageurs National Park, Minnesota: An application of the U.S. National Vegetation Classification. Applied Vegetation Science 10:361-374.

Frelich, L. E. 2002. Disturbance, stand development, and successional trajectories. *In* L. E. Frelich, editor. Forest dynamics and disturbance regimes: Studies from temperate evergreen-deciduous forests. Cambridge University Press, Cambridge, United Kingdom.

Frelich, L. E., and P. B. Reich. 1995. Spatial patterns and succession in a Minnesota southern-boreal forest. Ecological Monographs 65:325-346.

Gimmi, U., S. L. Schmidt, U. Gafvert, and V. C. Radeloff. 2009. Decreasing effectiveness of protected areas due to increasing development in the surroundings of U.S. National Park Service holdings after park establishment. National Resource Technical Report NPS/GLKN/NRTR–2009/178. National Park Service, Fort Collins, Colorado, USA.

Hammer, R. B., S. I. Stewart, R. L. Winkler, V. C. Radeloff, and P. R. Voss. 2004. Characterizing dynamic spatial and temporal residential density patterns from 1940-1990 across the North Central United States. Landscape and Urban Planning 69:183-199.

Heinselman, M. L. 1973. Fire in the virgin forests of the Boundary Waters Canoe Area, Minnesota. Quaternary Research 3:329-382.

Heinselman, M. L. 1996. The Boundary Waters Wilderness Ecosystem. University of Minnesota Press, Minneapolis, USA.

Heyerdahl, E. K., L. B. Brubaker, and J. K. Agee. 2001. Spatial controls of historical fire regimes: A multiscale example from the interior West, USA. Ecology 82:660-678.

Homer, C., C. Q. Huang, L. M. Yang, B. Wylie, and M. Coan. 2004. Development of a 2001 national land-cover database for the United States. Photogrammetric Engineering and Remote Sensing 70:829-840.

Host, G. E., and P. Meysembourg. 2010. Historic and recent landscape changes in relation to beaver activity in Voyageurs National Park, Minnesota, USA. Unpublished report to the

National Park Service Great Lakes Inventory and Monitoring Network and Voyageurs National Park.

Huang, C., S. N. Goward, J. G. Masek, N. Thomas, Z. Zhu, and J. E. Vogelmann. 2010. An automated approach for reconstructing recent forest disturbance history using dense Landsat time series stacks. Remote Sensing of Environment 114:183-198.

Jennings, M., D. Faber-Langendoen, R. Peet, O. Loucks, D. Glenn-Lewin, A. Damman, M. Barbour, R. Pfister, D. Grossman, D. Roberts, and others. 2004. Guidelines for describing associations and alliances of the U.S. National Vegetation Classification. The Ecological Society of America, Vegetation Classification Panel, Version 4.0.

Johnson, D. W. 1992. Effects of forest management on soil carbon storage. Water, Air, & Soil Pollution 64:83-120.

Johnson, D. W., and P. S. Curtis. 2001. Effects of forest management on soil C and N storage: Meta analysis. Forest Ecology and Management 140:227-238.

Johnston, C. A., and R. J. Naiman. 1990. Aquatic patch creation in relation to beaver population trends. Ecology 71:1617-1621.

Kennedy, R., A. Kirschbaum, U. Gafvert, P. Nelson, Z. Yang, W. Cohen, E. Pfaff, and B. Gholson. 2010. Landsat-based monitoring of landscape dynamics in the National Parks of the Great Lakes Inventory and Monitoring Network (Version 1.0). National Resource Report NPS/GLKN/NRR—2010/221, National Park Service, Fort Collins, Colorado, USA.

Kennedy, R. E., W. B. Cohen, and T. A. Schroeder. 2007. Trajectory-based change detection for automated characterization of forest disturbance dynamics. Remote Sensing of Environment 110:370-386.

Kennedy, R. E., P. A. Townsend, J. E. Gross, W. B. Cohen, P. Bolstad, Y. Q. Wang, and P. Adams. 2009. Remote sensing change detection tools for natural resource managers: Understanding concepts and tradeoffs in the design of landscape monitoring projects. Remote Sensing of Environment 113:1382-1396.

Kennedy, R. E., Z. Yang, and W. B. Cohen. In review. Detecting trends in forest disturbance and recovery using yearly Landsat time series: 1. LandTrendr - Temporal segmentation algorithms. Remote Sensing of Environment.

Kirschbaum, A., and U. Gafvert. 2010. Standard operating procedure #6: Lab validation of LandTrendr outputs. *In* R. Kennedy, A. Kirschbaum, U. Gafvert, P. Nelson, Z. Yang, W. Cohen, E. Pfaff, and B. Gholson. Landsat-based monitoring of landscape dynamics in the national parks of the Great Lakes Inventory and Monitoring Network (Version 1.0). Natural Resource Report NPS/GLKN/NRR—2010/221. National Park Service, Fort Collins, Colorado, USA.

Kirschbaum, A., and U. Gafvert. 2010. Standard operating procedure #7: Lab validation of LandTrendr outputs. *In* R. Kennedy, A. Kirschbaum, U. Gafvert, P. Nelson, Z. Yang, W. Cohen, E. Pfaff, and B. Gholson. Landsat-based monitoring of landscape dynamics in the national parks of the Great Lakes Inventory and Monitoring Network (Version 1.0). Natural Resource Report NPS/GLKN/NRR—2010/221. National Park Service, Fort Collins, Colorado, USA.

Koehler, G. M., and M. G. Hornocker. 1977. Fire effects on marten habitat in the Selway-Bitterroot Wilderness. The Journal of Wildlife Management 41:500-505.

Kurmis, V., S. L. Webb, and L. C. Merriam. 1986. Plant communities of Voyageurs National Park, Minnesota, U.S.A. Canadian Journal of Botany 64:531-540.

LeComte, D. 2010. North American Drought Monitor. National Oceanic and Atmospheric Administration. Drought indices and data available from (http://www.ncdc.noaa.gov/oa/ climate/monitoring/drought/nadm/indices.php). Accessed 19 July 2010.

Lyon, L. J., M. H. Huff, R. G. Hooper, E. S. Telfer, D. S. Schreiner, and J. K. Smith. 2000. Wildland fire in ecosystems: Effects of fire on fauna. General Technical Report RMRS-GTR-42 (Vol.1). USDA Forest Service, Rocky Mountain Research Station, Ogden, Utah, USA.

McGranahan, D. A. 1999. Natural amenities drive rural population change. Agricultural Economic Report No. 781, U.S. Department of Agriculture, Economic Research Service, Washington, D.C., USA

Moser, K. W., M. H. Hansen, M. D. Nelson, S. J. Crocker, C. H. Perry, B. Schulz, and C. W. Woodall. 2007. After the blowdown: A resource assessment of the Boundary Waters Canoe Area Wilderness, 1999-2003. General Technical Report NRS-7, USDA Forest Service, Northern Research Station, Newton Square, Pennsylvania, USA.

Nabuurs, G. J., R. Päivinen, R. Sikkema, and G. M. J. Mohren. 1997. The role of European forests in the global carbon cycle–A review. Biomass and Bioenergy 13:345-358.

National Interagency Coordination Center Predictive Services. 2010. National wildland significant fire potential outlook – May through August 2010. National Interagency Fire Center. Data and maps available from (http://www.nifc.gov/nicc/predictive/outlooks/ outlooks.htm). Accessed 19 July 2010.

Ojakangas, R. W., and C. L. Matsch. 1982. Minnesota's Geology. University of Minnesota Press, Minneapolis, USA.

Route, B., and J. Elias. 2007. Long-term ecological monitoring plan: Great Lakes Inventory and Monitoring Network. Natural Resource Report NPS/GLKN/NRR—2001/001. National Park Service, Fort Collins, Colorado, USA.

Rowe, J. S., and G. W. Scotter. 1973. Fire in the boreal forest. Quaternary Research 3:444-464.

Sanders, S., S. E. Johnson, and D. M. Waller. 2008. Vegetation monitoring protocol: Great Lakes Inventory & Monitoring Network. Natural Resource Report NPS/GLKN/NRR—2008/056. National Park Service, Fort Collins, Colorado, USA.

Scheller, R. M., D. J. Mladenoff, T. R. Crow, and T. A. Sickley. 2005. Simulating the effects of fire reintroduction versus continued fire absence on forest composition and landscape structure in the Boundary Waters Canoe Area, northern Minnesota, USA. Ecosystems 8:396-411.

Schroeder, T. A., W. B. Cohen, C. H. Song, M. J. Canty, and Z. Q. Yang. 2006. Radiometric correction of multi-temporal Landsat data for characterization of early successional forest patterns in western Oregon. Remote Sensing of Environment 103:16-26.

Smith, D. W., and R. O. Peterson. 1988. The effects of regulated lake levels on beaver in Voyageurs National Park, Minnesota. U.S. Department of Interior, National Park Service. Research/Resources Management Report #MWR-11. National Park Service files, International Falls, Minnesota, USA.

Svancara, L., P. Budde, and J. Gross. 2009a. Measure development summary: Population and housing. National Park Service, Office of Inventory, Monitoring, and Evaluation, Fort Collins, Colorado, USA.

Svancara, L., T. Philippi, and J. Gross. 2009b. Measure development summary: Roads. National Park Service, Office of Inventory, Monitoring, and Evaluation, Fort Collins, Colorado, USA.

Svancara, L., and M. Story. 2009. Measure development summary: Land cover/land use. National Park Service, Office of Inventory, Monitoring, and Evaluation, Fort Collins, Colorado, USA.

Vogelmann, J. E., T. L. Sohl, P. V. Campbell, and D. M. Shaw. 1998. Regional land cover characterization using Landsat thematic mapper data and ancillary data sources. Environmental Monitoring and Assessment 51:415-428.

White, M. A., and G. E. Host. 2003. Changes in disturbance frequency, age and patch structure from pre-Euro-American to settlement to present in northcentral and northeastern Minnesota. Minnesota Forest Resources Council Report LT-1203a, St. Paul, USA.

White, M. A., and G. E. Host. 2008. Forest disturbance frequency and patch structure from pre-European settlement to present in the Mixed Forest Province of Minnesota, USA. Canadian Journal of Forest Research 38:2212-2226.

White, M. K., S. T. Gower, and D. E. Ahl. 2005. Life cycle inventories of roundwood production in northern Wisconsin: Inputs into an industrial forest carbon budget. Forest Ecology and Management 219:13-28.

Wolter, P. T., C. A. Johnston, and G. J. Niemi. 2006. Land use land cover change in the U.S. Great Lakes basin 1992 to 2001. Journal of Great Lakes Research 32:607-628.

Wolter, P. T., and M. A. White. 2002. Recent forest cover type transitions and landscape structural changes in northeast Minnesota. Landscape Ecology 17:133-155.

Woodall, C. W., and L. M. Nagel. 2007. Downed woody fuel loading dynamics of a large-scale blowdown in northern Minnesota, U.S.A. Forest Ecology and Management 247:194-199.

Wulder, M. A., J. A. Dechka, M. A. Gillis, J. E. Luther, R. J. Hall, and A. Beaudoin. 2003. Operational mapping of the land cover of the forested area of Canada with Landsat data: EOSD Land Cover Program. Forestry Chronicle 79:1075-1083.

NPS 172/105049, July 2010